Memory and Heaven

ooooooooooooooooooo

To Chris—
Very good to meet
you!

Best,
the other Chri

Also by CHRISTOPHER HOWELL:

SWEET AFTON

SEA CHANGE

THOUGH SILENCE: THE LING WEI TEXTS

WHY SHOULDN'T I

THE CRIME OF LUCK

Memory and Heaven

‹‹‹‹‹‹‹‹‹‹‹‹‹‹‹‹‹

CHRISTOPHER
HOWELL

Christoph Howell

EWU
P·R·E·S·S

Eastern Washington University Press
Cheney, Washington 1996

EASTERN WASHINGTON UNIVERSITY PRESS
MS-133 / Eastern Washington University / 526 5th Street / Cheney, WA 99004-2431

ISBN 0-910055-27-0 [Cloth]
ISBN 0-910055-28-9 [Paper]

Printed in the United States of America
02 01 00 99 98 97 96   5 4 3 2 1

LIBRARY OF CONGRESS CATALOGING-IN-PUBLICATION DATA

Howell, Christopher.
    Memory and heaven / Christopher Howell.
        p.   cm.
    ISBN 0-910055-27-0 (*hardcover*). — ISBN 0-910055-28-9 (*pbk.*)
    1. Title.
PS3558.0897M46 1996
811'.54—DC20   95-42584
                                                                      CIP

Acknowledgments appear on page 79

The text was set in a digitized version of Caslon.
Book design by Terry Bain.
Cover design by John Smith.

This book is dedicated to Barbara, Emma, and Evan; and to Bill Stafford, to whom I did not get to say goodbye.

CONTENTS

PART I

Love and Justice

"In some of the heart's business there is
really no net gain. Let someone who knows
tell you."

—RICHARD FORD

The Bride of Long Division

Water spiders dissemble the light and spillage
of day
and my ribbons and portraits agree
that if what goes around comes around
like whips of the angels, I must be
divided just to live
as rivers live
with the moving sticks and leaves and tumbling
stones. Just to live I must have the bride
who wears me like shoes
taking their separate ignorant steps
toward the water spider's palace of edges and seams.
If I love her, how will I know it
from love of myself? If she makes for me
a perfect tabulation of the indivisible
which it is thought only the beasts achieve,
how will I bear the duplicity of touching
her again? How can the shadow
go on without the self to dance with
across the tense surface of mind
while something else looks up with adoration
from a deeper place and something else
comes home to reeds and lilies, groom and last remainder,
describing it all?

ooooo

Alienation

When the alien spoke of his planet
it was with an ache so profound
I forgot he was going to kill me.
I looked into the chrome and blue
glaciers of his eyes and said,
It's all right, I know how it is
when you're away from home,
when time and distance coalesce
like the speed of light
and freeze your heart coordinates.

He didn't have a heart. He didn't
even have toes, but he liked the sentiment
and said I'd not be killed and eaten
after all
but only changed.
I thought how often change had seemed
the one salvation. But when he said it
I woke to the sensation of singing
under water, while air diminished, slowly,
like hope.

The creature, in his lance of a ship,
was soon the distant sparkle of alienation
itself: roads that will not converge,
singers who cannot close their mouths.
Was this the beginning? Who can say
where or when it began in him?
I just woke and there was this voice-like
distance
between myself and the things I loved.

From the Lover of Violets

You say I have come to town at last
but I've not, I've gone away.
This is the joy of violets I wanted to give you
at the precise point of your vulnerability.
"It will be like spreading them on a grave,"
I used to say. "It will be like halving a lemon
and throwing both halves away."
What's before you may look like my body.
And those fingers searching you out
probably seem like mine, feel like
the way I used to ease them
into you. But I'm not there, you see;
I've taken leave
on some island that has fallen
off the charts of navigators and priests.
With a lifetime supply of self
I have arrived at my station, alone
and therefore unexpected. I have a violet soufflé
in one hand (looking for you). In the other
I carry the list of everything I meant to do
before leaving, and everything I meant to say.
It is unreadable now, of course, something to do
with salt. But one item was, "Kiss her and kiss her
until the pale green centaur emerges from her breast
again." Did I ever tell you how much I loved that?
Another item was, "Don't cry, it's only your life.
You'll get over it." An indirect action, but
I had been looking forward to it
until I forgot.
Another item was, "Place your palm along your face
and whisper as though she were telling you she would never

turn you into a raw and stupid absence
again." That one was so difficult
I forgot it while writing it down,
just as I am forgetting this.
Just as I am forgetting you and the reasons
for my confusion and for the great rivers
of liquid salt dissolving everything I meant to do
before I left; including perhaps the leaving itself.
But we don't know that yet and the violets
are beautiful
and look, look they are part of my hand!

Blade

That woman whose face is a blade
comes out of the corn
singing. She has swayed in the breath
of so many arms she is almost a willow
the color of June.
And so many eyes have gazed
at her nakedness
and known the beautiful madness of horses
dozing in mist under an apple tree
that she almost tosses her mane
and lets sunlight caress her
as it does the corn.
Wherever she goes now, because she belongs
everywhere, there will be green collisions
and a sky that might clear again
and water cold and bright like a blade,
like a good life falling to earth.

Denial

So, you've taken to eating live birds,
spilling the gore and suffering cries
down over your lacey cuffs and collar.
What makes a difference now
after this primly vicious predation

and the shock on faces of the passersby?
If you say you were born at the crux
of a soft rapine and vanishment,
perhaps the new guardian police
will grant you an orange

or another live bird shaped like an orange
or perhaps only the feet of some unlucky crow
who flew up so suddenly from ice
her body became a stranger
lifted forever into the exhaustion of flight.

Is winter to blame for this
feather wedged between your teeth,
this absence of the little girl
who drew cattails and sang
like a canary?

Your dreamy, red-lipped life has come upon us
like a nightmare we're ashamed of, one of those
in which hideous desires bloom in our fingers
and loins, and we offer everything we have
that it should not be part of us.

The Blue Flight Back/Adam's Song

Broken as I was I wanted
to say blue
was always the stupid luck
we call perfection.
I used to drive a Ford
so blue
the sky desired it. Once I kissed
a blue cup
smaller than your hand forgetting
all other hands
in the grip of itself.
When I was twelve
I met a blue spruce angel
blue as carpenters' chalk
blue as rain in the memory
of desert men.

Broken as I was I thought
the decade should pay, should float
with pay like a liquid extinction
swimming a stroke so blue
the very hope of water would be a sad
and sadly falling bird too blue
to fly. So, when I fell
I broke, and
broken as I was the purely blue
mountain lakes and saxophones
became a kind of gasp
abandoned like a love letter
in the trash, exactly.

But as I was
broken
implied the hope of the broken, the sky-
colored vein that swears mountains
are its nuptial contentments
dismantled at grieving cost; as only the needle
dismantles, as memory
dismantles knowledge stabbed in
to blood winding like a Ford through distance
perfectly blue
toward the perfect death from which it starts.

Elegy at the Onset of Winter

—*for* JAMES WRIGHT

I love you and wish you grace,
dead apple, empty space.
You were fair enough, almost blond,
in any case, and I come alone
at dark to call you friend and good
deceiver of the Devil's face.
If we touched, you could come back
to be the wind-teased cottonwoods
lining the tangled field at dawn.
You could come down
from the bridge that bears you,
gray as breath, aloft
and singing like a single paper rose
because you hear the ancient palm
of light unfolding for a song
called *Whisper, Were You Ever Here?*
or where in the blinding quick
of Summer have you gone?

Four Solitudes

There were four of them
successively alone in their passage
along that road
no longer much more than an invitation to travel.
Courting the same woman
perhaps, singing into the same well
by which echo and reflection mask themselves
with what they must return,
the four of them only once passed by
those grassy hills, along that overgrown thought
between two lines of maples.

That all four were the same
man, that each of him beseeched the birds
for something simply every name forgets, that each
had grown a crippled wing and didn't know it,
can be told at last, at least. But why
follow this way, this unused valley track
among the rust of barns
and wagon wheels? "Why not," they would say,
"We're so hidden by wind we can't collect the light
that lets things live. Time follows this curve
of space and moon swings her secret pearl
like water obeying the grain of wood. So here we are."

Nothing came of their journey; there were four,
each the same, drifting where they might
one day be imagined, awakened by the glaring
mind's eye and then the mind, probing and blinking
with wonder. That is, life is the appearance of unity
in series, whether you see

or it sees you, every time you reconstruct
its watchfulness and let the new guidon choose
the road you chose before, its trees, sounds
bear no witness
and dance heartless as rocks.
What's it all mean, I suppose. Sleeper, who's to know
the ear of the cello and the beech tree bud? I could only
kiss you if I knew which one of me you're not. It's clear
as the four of them eloping, each with Descartes
on his lips
and the supposition of loss draped over him
like a robe of power.

The Ecstasy of Ceasing to Know

I painted my hand on the window
and that part of the glass ceased to know itself
because with windows form is its own recognition
and the portrait of my hand was alien
formal hypothesis. When I painted
the same hand on an arm
of the blue chair, I thought I heard breathing
and for a moment supposed also a spot of lighter blue
weaving a slow ironic signature over the cushion.
But soon my disruption of the chair's being
and its subsequent brief tango at the margins of simulation
passed into the known body and fabric of CHAIR
and I fit my living hand
to the image, which remained quite helpless
before the mockery implied of this gesture.
Then I desired to paint my hand against the cat
but he discerned some pallor in the silence of my shoes
and he bolted
and even now, weeks later, remains aloof
so that I doubt the project shall engage him more directly.
Still, on a back wall of his brain a terror
strokes him, inevitably
in the shape of my hand. Well, I moved on
to the appliances
with decent though short-lived result; owing to the systematic
interference of current, an liquid presence
the praxis of which is related to singing
in the very sense in which appliances are not.
I took note of this and, cuing on the whiteness
of refrigerators in general (and of mine most particularly),
I discovered the large, flat articulation

ooooo

of my hand itself *pretending* "refrigerator."
Such challenge: to simulate the intentional ellipsis of form
unintentionally conceiving only self when there is no only self!
Well, the work glides forward
furiously, in some zones; in others the photo-intimation of stasis
fingerpaints Plato with shadows palpable as rock—
which it would be possible to break up and carry away.
Therefore, clearly, no hierarchy exists between subject
and object so that not only must the hand be painted *on* its mirrored
original, it must also (I see at last) be painted *by* this same hand.
Here I have encountered a near hallelujah
of telemetric fishhooks and a piquant ignorance
for which no language serves and by which I begin, dimly, to see
that non-shape, so familiar to my cat, as a ballet
of opaque, perfected, and dozing subject/object calculations
which, yes, are (I feel it!) painting me
over and over like a pencil
drawing a cartoonist who has recently ceased to know
the shapes of humility and science as they coalesce in him
and this ecstasy is born without image or thought
of image, without hope of any kind.

The Abomination of Fallen Things

Look at them in pieces
all over the floor.
Who would have guessed
their ability to float temporary
or their bodies fragile as dragonflies
of glass. I kneel
and scan the sad assortment
of bent struts, doorposts, and shoe-shaped
devices. Several zeros
still wobble in circles
like cast off hubcaps. A half signature,
"Carmen," crawls through the wreckage
looking for its other half.
The whole thing is abominable!
I want to cover it with my coat
or create a room
in which such things never occur
then go there
and improve myself till I can re-emerge
and take up my cleansed place
among those special men who can stand
to look at what they've done.

Dialectic/From Three Windows

I. FOR THE FISHERMEN

Rain and gray shoulders of the sea.
I think of Jesus walking away
against the horizon; those in the boat
open-mouthed,
almost angry with astonishment.
And in the bar afterwards, of course,
he lets them tell it.
But his face is the calm water
hiding everything. "Come on, Jesus,
how do you *do* that stuff?"
He isn't saying. He just sips his wine
then water then wine
and thinks about weather in the age
to come; how dark it will be,
how far men will have to walk—and over
what water—for a good joke
or a blessing.

2. WITH THE DISTANCE

The birds of leaves are waving
as if they had had no voices.
It is their way with the distance
which has no voice
but only the shapes, sounds
of wings, footsteps, water hurrying off.
So, if I hold a bird of leaves
fluttering like a moth
in my closed hand, I will not be required
to read aloud the journey I begin to see
in your straight, strong body.
The landscape there is miles of hawthorn trees,
blossoms elegantly clothing their knives
as though beauty doesn't hurt
when we try to hold it, rocking,
waiting for the strange green birds to sing.

3. AT FRIDAY HARBOR NEAR CHRISTMA

On an ice and salt encrusted piling
the cormorant has been all morning
as if crucified,
drying his wings in the snow.
Black beacon to the slow bobbing
boats asleep here for months,
he is without sadness and does not know
whose loneliness clings to him
through a window across the water.

Oh one of these days
when I have shed my body, dark bird,
I will walk out to you
and sit quietly
enjoying the morning, the white dazzle
of it falling through my outstretched wings.

Blessing's Precision

And we emerged from the treeline
and came upon a lion, bleeding
and a man kissing the wounds
from which the blood whispered out.
Some of us wanted to kill the lion
quickly, then the man
and to write down how this was done,
how a voice commanded it.
Some of us wept for the lion
and for the love the man must have felt
to bend down like that, like an angel,
and do what he was doing.
Some of us thought we could see home
in the bloody grass and in the stillness
of the man's mouth saying a thing
no one but the dying
lion was close enough to hear.

Finally we decided to make a ritual
for passing by a wounded lion and an angel
when you come upon them
by accident
and one of them is watching his heart's blood
run bitterly away, in spite of the sweetness
it had always brought before.
And so we held our faces up against the sky
and said our benedictions
and gave up each a bead
from our own red estuaries. And a caress
we might have saved
we placed in the man's palm

till his hands overflowed with little stones
smooth as a lion's ear.

Then we left the both of them there, dying
I suppose, and many of us have been speechless
since then, curiously
simplified in a kind of sunlight asleep
in a kind of shade. Since then
we have begun to build this rose,
this village of our days
where every breathing thing must be received
and tended, because mercy, now, locks our arms
out wide, and nothing, not even happiness,
is ever turned away.

PART II

Flights and Ships

Tiller of waves or whatever, woman or man,
Mother of roots or father of diamonds,
Look: I am nothing.
I do not even have ashes to rub into my eyes.

—JAMES WRIGHT

The God in Central Park

If one god has risen from ailanthus
in Central Park, rubbing his eyes,
no one has seen him. No one has heard
the odd five-note amazement strike
evening branches as he pipes
his ancient themes. The world
will not change for him again. Old magic,
old beauty, what are they? Who will see
now the faun look back, trailing
a spray of stars?

If a god, an old strange god, has risen
somewhere in Central Park,
he is alone
and wrong. That nymph he has pursued
over time and all the seas
has changed from reeds to ashes,
surely. Surely the dark stacks
spill her down over the god's white shoulders
as he turns to stone
and the cop, blue and weary and public, passes
without a glance.

Night Flight Letter to Weldon Kees Found Wadded Up inside a Lucky Strike Wrapper

I'm writing you after all these years
because people keep saying there is this
kinship of sensibility. Flying over Kansas
now, at a dizzy cloudless elevation, I can't see it.
But you with your cigarette and mustache
and your swept-back Nathanael West darkness so deeply
in love with the cynical tide of things, I can see
them OK in this book—which I admit isn't mine.
I'm your age now is another reason
I'm contacting you. Word is you jumped
at 41; and here I am
clinging to every shred of time, by God, and wondering,
Weldon, how to live,
how to stay for one more kiss
in the arms of such mystery of heart
I can't manage either. So
I was a PI and a tough
character,
arguably ("Don't try me," was, anyway, always my advice).
So I loved without any particular restraint or shame.
I love you, too; does that make us similar? Did you
really jump, throw it all
into "them shark-infested waves" like a prom queen
who's gotten old? Come on,
tell me I'm wrong (all of us
must be) as Ptolemy was wrong: that is
because the world is not logical
is it? Think
how many have died like the solitary
tapping pattern buried in Mexico City rubble for days
while the crews dug and wept?

Was it you, Weldon, lost in the hours of earth;
plummeting into the night smile
like a bird? Well, I think
you're a shit for going off like that, on purpose,
leaving us lonely for your profile, for someone
like you but older
and hopeful. Not as dead.

Kipling Visits Portland and the West

It was a different place Kipling saw
when he came, almost a century ago, for the fishing,
he said.

A few buildings, rude and crowded waterfront shops
bulging with produce and meats. He stood amazed
at how things changed in price
according to the weather, how what seemed the right equipage
for his stepping forth was, like a secret, nowhere
to be had.

His native guide, the graceful androgyne in red
and yellow silks, could find no elephants
and settled for a mule
hired from Laursen's Livery on Salmon Street.
They must have been a sight, setting off
turbaned and pith-helmeted, all "rum up and steady there!"
the whole nineteenth century mounted and loaded for ridicule
under the snowtops.

But how clear that northern air! How oddly beautiful
to fish for days in veins of frigid flowing glass
and catch no thing but solitude
and respite from the world's passing him by, unaware
that he looked back over his shoulder, over the sea

and saw something constructed by a gentleman with long
very clean hands, a garden of sleepy tigers
with boys wandering by canals and tossing pignuts at the swans.
But never mind. His line rode the dazzling flash and shadow
of the Clackamas

through occasional spates of rain, night silences,
small reports of pine pitch in the campfire flames.

ooooo

It is raining as I write this, looking out, thinking
of the Road to Mandalay and of the soldier who went too far
ever to return, though he was English and wanted to.

Through the lace of this rainfall the city across the river
glows and glitters with sunlight like a new-washed orange.

ooooo

Kipling left after a few days and never came back.
This is what we all do when time runs off without us, we pretend
living is a matter of place
and we mumble some old rhyme and go off like kings
of a country we are sure to find
after the rain
or the snow or the long road
full of solitary soldiers who are never going home.

Streets

Catullus, returning late
from the "sun-drenched farmlands of Nicaea,"
saw a hook of smoke lean
to the pink goblet
fallen from a window and smashed.
It was the hook
mourning makes, he said, after
the hand has broken faith
with what it beautifully held,
after the good air
cracks its jaw against the table.
                              Then
five silent Phrygians drifted by
rowing
and scattering little boat-like meditations
from The Book Of Odd Number.
                              Then
he heard the weeper, Flavius,
banding his ankles as he tittered and wept
about mendacity
in his lover's verbs.
                    Then
Catullus thought this night swerves
like a girl loosening her robe
while one man watches
and another paces the crooked paving stones
and longs to watch. Then
Catullus was all night in the streets
lit by smoke of a step disrobed
and shattered as a precious cup
can be. Then he was another man

and another;
            bleeding like this
bleeding like this, he said. *Imagine.*
Then he let go.

Everyday Dramatics: An Historical Tale

At Count Pilchek's garden gala
as the roses were waltzing
and swans parsed the white sighs of metaphor
she, in yards of taffeta, approached her lover,
Dronishkin, and curtsied
like a lake to his mountain.
Would he lend his dagger to a special dance?
Good.
And she placed it flat, point down
between her breasts
so he would have to hold her close, now,
he would have to remember his pride
grinding and grinding the edges of blade
so a slightest accidental slippage of its finger
would bring blood to anything but stones.
He would have to hold firmly
but with respect, otherwise who could tell
with blades and women? So distinct in the beginning, yet
through carelessness or chance
might not one mark the other? Or (Perish *this*, Sasha!)
might they not merge
in a way
and turn against the callous innocence of certain men like points
of departure?
And wasn't it grand to speak thus and move, one being,
through the pools of torch and candle glow?
And didn't he believe, now, what she would surely do
if the woman waiting in loose silks in a manse
on Ilyakovich Street
did not go on waiting till her sex became the tempered

cutting edge of which
it has ever been bad luck to make a gift?

He let her bleed
until her bodice resembled a swatch of fresh
carnations and she fainted,
just as she had hoped, in front of everyone; though
Sauros, the servant, stumbled
and drew off attention with a brilliant curse.
Lenin was there,
spitting in the punch, and Dronishkin saw
the time for everyday dramatics would not last.
A practical man, he did not give up the other
mistress. He went on
changing garments four times daily, observing
the balance of sounds
tinkling in opulent rooms heavy with cognac and cigar.
Smug, without scars or hope, he went on
secreting his jeweled dagger in the necks of the palace guard,
in the crests on yellowing invitations
later set alight with the furniture and curtains
and an uncle's violin on the last night
of winter
when he would stand gazing out at the snow's reluctance
and the red signatures melting into it like swans
turned inside out.

The Christian Science Minotaur

He is half bull
and half book
and he eats broccoli, mostly,
with sauce. He says, "I wish
I could kill something
or smoke."
But his room is only open
10 to 4 and nothing is allowed
in but eyeglasses and the curious
who stare straight at him and yawn.
When nights get bad
and he has again read through
himself without solving the riddle
of a life without hospitals
or booze, he lifts the venetian blinds
and broods out through the gold-leaf lettering,
and thinks, "Surely they will send youths
or a clever boy with string."
And surely they do not send him anything
but the thin, impalpable subscriptions
no good to eat. And he *is* hungry,
though his soul, it is said, is stuffed
with all that's good for him.

The News

Before Confucius said "No" it was Chinese custom to immolate living dog, servants, concubines and wife along with the wide-eyed and carefully painted corpse of the nobleman. The Other World was thought to be far away and glittering with necessities only a peasant or an eunuch or a woman would go forth to all alone, like a fish battling great rivers on the way to death.

It was widely reported that sacrificed women wept exclusively for the dearly dead, never for that savagery death had ignited all around them. Even the dogs and horses, it was said, mooned only for the master sent alarmingly off ahead of them, and so, with the wisdom of good beasts, were anxious for the flames to scorch apart the veil dividing flesh from light and let them down, free, on the eternal paths of servitude and love.

As fire crept up the racks of faggots, chewing faster and faster like a famished menace, some claimed figures in the blaze kowtowed, smiling bodhisatvah-like into their last earthly moments or clapping with expectation. Actually, Confucius tells us, they screamed, like nothing else but creatures burning in the ruins of their lives, so that no amount of mourning brought relief to those who heard them, everyone shuddering for terrible death, desperately, as today we shudder at the small starving faces brought to us in the evening as we eat. And those watchers long ago, before Confucius, said finally there is nothing we can do until a wise man comes to tell us, "This is unseemly. This is mad."

Werewolf at Dawn, the Female Moon Having Left Him

Why so much hapless struggle
against the gravity of desire?
His questions are grainy bones.
Even his heart, rubber thing silly
about blessings (but false), is every
tired beast coming off its shift.
Even She, delirium sear letting in light
where no light knows its way, even She
is no lollipop, he can see. Just stone,
miles of it and miles away.

Rolling over in the tangled bed
he can see She has no care either
for the mist that fills a man, his swamp
of dangers and sudden flights. And alone
he is what he is (the shudder, high wail,
bloody ligaments and terror in the park),
a life tasting of silver and bruises
which shine while no wind stirs
the curtains and endless night
glimmers behind a cloud.

The Contemporary Theorist Alone at Dusk in His Chair by the Sea

The peaceful agony of cats
waiting for supper on a wide bright porch
says be wordless, if you like. Zachary Taylor;
the Dalton Gang; the republic of vanished Romans
drifting in robes
down to the Tiber to observe the conjugations of late sun
on water: these are the same
silent glisten you, hand on a shut book, speak to now.
Tell it to stop implying transcendence and the shameless
presence of gods whose love is only the inexplicable
cats filled with summer light.
Tell it you've tried feeling holy when days or seasons
turn puzzled faces through the air
like random beams of Sanskrit, so pure
they translate themselves. Insist
you'll not be bled
by the vaunted longing-to-define that births such slow and ugly
necessary thoughts. You've been to the mountain, say,
and the other mountain
and they were about the same. Say what's *here* is the strangeness
filling everything
and unable to talk about it. Of course, words are wasted
on the water, no matter how metaphorical. And naturally you'll
admit
(though not privately) its grace
is like a brother; something you never asked for,
something like you
with a language referring always and only to itself.

ooooo

45

Out of the Body

Alone in my gray sleeves
above lily fields and hills where green
nearly devours the sheep,
I think of Wordsworth's silhouette
fixed in the scene somewhere, pensively
replacing logos with daffodils
and beasts.

If I've heard the latest news correctly,
all over earth our light has grown insufficient
to its century. But the world
from Wordsworth's hill
could catch your wrist bone and bring lamps
out of us both. I don't mean that
as a gesture, *best of luck*,

but as an actual report. In fact, gazing
over the calm nape of valley I think
some hurt would leave the world forever
if we let it go. This is one of the lilies
at mind's edge where Wordsworth entered
his astonishment so beautifully he found
himself part of Nature and Nature part of God.

I know, immortality and death seem distinct
even here among the sheep and so much green
grass, sky, and lilies (again). But time
heals all, they say, even the wounds of time itself.
So maybe William is here waiting, democratically,
to begin the new, perfected discourse upon soul
and breath, or to simply shake our hands or wave

as the moon comes up or down
and the sheep suddenly know that
some of us have disappeared into the blue
above our bodies.

Talk with the Moon

Tutto è pace e silenzio, e tutto posa
il mondo, e più di lor non si ragiona.

—GIACOMO LEOPARDI

Leopardi asked the moon if it, too, would be silent
all his life.
After the grass and stones refused his graceful inclinations
he had tacked all hope of magic to the moon because
beauty, he said, privately, is the failure of realism.
But that night when he asked
the moon was real enough
and Leopardi, looking up, turned his ankle in a rut
and low-bridged his nose against a bough that over-hung the way
he had to follow then.
He cursed, and who could blame him? I know the dazzle
and simplicity of voice he longed for
but had not wished to talk about
earlier
when his wife, tired of his pacing the house, said, "Get
the hell out of here, why don't you? Go down to the bar
with Ugo or Alessandro or Giuseppe or go up to your room
and write some poetry!"
Though he had no wife, of course,
this sword-thrust made the tang of metal bloom
on Leopardi's tongue. How could he say
to her
the soul's night vision would burn out in heat and blare
of such bonfires
banked against the ordinary cold? Well, so, playing it out,
he put on his hat with the long purple feather
and stumbled into Florentine moonlight
like a foppish drunk.

What does it matter where
he went, his puzzled up-cast face seeking a voice
and all its secret fellowship ascending
with the ancient stars?

What does it matter? He knew where he was; he opened
the door and found himself, an old poet, dead
a century and more, smiling as the moon's mouth moved
to say, "All is peace and silence, and the world
rests entirely, and we do not speak of them now."

You Sailed Away, Oh Yes You Did

for ADAM HAMMER, 1949-1984

Against the sky, against the water sailing away
was not as blue as snow beside a trough
from which a naked girl has stepped moments before
she is imagined. Sailing away was never so vivid
as hammer marks in the door jamb of a shed, either.
And I never saw you shining a stone on your sleeve,
dropping it into the twinkly phosphorescence.
And you didn't lunge for the throat of a new book
about esthetics and the average man who sails away
in a Ford, the last of it assembling around him
as he studies his charts and holds one finger moistly up
in windless afternoon.

Where was he sailing to? wonder the wounded mammals.
Certainly none of this occurred in Florida
or in the nautical vacancy of a stowaway's tongue
frozen by laughter. Certainly I sailed some way
with him, or you; regardless of head-on Fords
falling into the side mirror of a night average as dots.
Certainly as you sail the undressed sea
empty of owls, the grass around me is rusting, collapsing
because it is so stupidly ashore
caressing its sad laces, knowing you've gone.
Like a proton parking meter filled with mischief and stars;
like a fig bar the rain disapproves of;
like a window becoming a zip-lock bag when no one is listening;
like a man dressing his grief in a clown suit
you've gone.

Ships

Holding their secret histories
like Bibles, ships come in long slow bass notes,
announcing a sadness so profound
even sharp night distances clutch
against the moans of wind. Even the water
almost forgives them purpose, cargo,
and the buoyancy which seems to it unnatural.

Now in the last evening hour
the very thought of loneliness is terrifying.
Yet the ships sail out
and never know we are here under bare trees
near channels, dark in the starlight
striking us like rain; will never hear us
calling out that we have come to the end of land.

PART III

Memory and Heaven

If the world were only pain and logic,
who would want it.

—MARY OLIVER

Lines from a Heaven Imagined by Peaches

Of course it was blue, and when I removed
what was left of my withered pit of a soul,
I turned around there and knew I was home;
or that, at least, the road would go no farther.
If from the truth of this arrival
I took the air like some great beaming angel
whose talent is flying into deepest privacy
where even God knocks before entering
(unless She's angry), who could blame or ask
my reasons? Anyway, I couldn't help it: suddenly
my eyes were solid blue and blind to that
lurching fruitcart castle I'd been hitched to.
My days were come into a new and breathing house
where every door stood open and blue hands
reached out to take me in.

The Record Player

In the next room Barbara listens to ballads; familiar,
inoffensive phrasings discovered at a used record shop
on Hawthorn. The woman's voice is low and strong

with its charmed lights and losses winking and the
moon sailing off by itself somewhere above the rain
and other forms of weeping for the Earth.

Then she swings brightly south, Caribbean, where love
is a thoughtless shimmering absence of decay we think
we must, by suffering, have earned. Occasionally

she mentions cormorants and the color blue as it must
have been for Columbus, bent above his imaginary
charts, hollering at his first officer, "Not now!

Not now! Can't you see I'm plotting a course!" Finally
she brings a song of sleep and wordlessness and the
machine lifts its arm coldly out of her voice,

sinking now into the dark vinyl like a djin charmed
back into a golden lamp that isn't really gold. If the
voice returns

it will come because we call it, by devices; it will never
bring itself. In this it differs from events; the artifactual
aplomb of war, for instance,

seems avoidable only in retrospect as men in
immaculate pinstripe move among the smoking arms
and heads, counting and thinking we didn't ask

for this one, boy. We didn't even know it was inside
us all this time, pretending to be a song we had
grown tired of

or forgotten as we forget the moon's dark other hand,
the one that points, naturally, toward the emptiness
and salutes.

The Ride

for T.L.

You probably don't remember,
it was years ago. You and I and Amorosi
and David Lyon rode down to Springfield
in the back of Tremblay's rattletrap van.

                         You sat
with a pint of peach brandy in a bag
on your knees
and said nothing
the whole loud careening way
along the back roads from Belchertown.
I thought you disdainful of us
maybe, or too drunk to know
we wanted you to speak

                as we spoke
about the evening or the road
or the ghostly broken milltowns we passed through
or anything at all.

                But you just sat
under your lank whitish hair,
tippling, not even looking up
when we hit the possum, all its kittens
hung from it like a string of bells.
Tremblay nearly cried, rocking
like a bear in the headlight beams,
shaking his head above that quivering
heap of blood and eyes.
You didn't get out with the rest of us
to console or lead him back
so the journey could go on.

                When we arrived
and piled out to find the appointed room,

you said, "It's cold tonight"
to no one
and I saw my judgment of you
a broken worried thing, like so much
of what we knew then
in those days after the war.

                      You simply hadn't cared
to speak.
You had your thoughts
and the rest of us were just the rest of us
borne together through a single night,
no one knowing it would never end
and never be the same; no one but you
knowing how much the voice can cost, how wrongly
it can take you
into the path of a transfixing lie, its headlights
coming on
monstrous and too beautiful for words.

The Pipes of Oblivion

Nansen went up on deck and saw a bird-shaped
constellation
flying and singing as it flew.
It didn't bother him; in those days
Norwegians often saw that sort of thing.

He took out his pipe, whacked it on the rail
to clear the bowl,
then wandered aft, thinking, "What astonishing notation
the footfall brings. This must be oblivion!"
It was a giddy time,

the ice was taking them to where the North began

and it was likely they would die
(as the grim joke went) of having no place else to go.
The bird shape sang again. O well, he ordered the mate
to turn in
and stood the rest of the watch himself,

letting smoke rings lift into the icy arctic wheel
and thinking how little time
mattered
to a ship or man stuck fast
in a voyage
even imaginary gods could not recall the object of.

Everything

Ponce de Leon, whose youth was all too short,
scrawled his name and number in the Book
Of Certain Sorrows by wanting everything
to stay, always, just the way it no longer was.

His fine moustaches and silver mirror,
his fingers buffed like little marble candlesticks,
the heart-shaped box where he sent hope to lie
against itself, waiting out the miracle he was sure
hacked its way toward him through the mangrove swamps,
using prayer beads as navigational aids; anyone
could read the signs.
                    And he had a funny,
rounded sort of name, "Ponce," falsely intricate,
like a Swiss watch made of chocolate.
Also he was small and getting smaller
as the quest went on: three times he had his armor
taken in so that, approaching a pool or bubbling spring,
he would project that no-nonsense manly form
Indians in Florida, ever since, have known to mark
a magnitude of lunacy from which to "hush" and wink
and tippy-toe away.
                    In the end, too, he sang—
to keep his spirit tuned and ready to receive the whole
hog mysteries of never-ending day—and his men sang with him
so he wouldn't seem so mad to them
and the birds observed these clanking choristers
slogging fiercely, eyes on the sun, stooping
here and there to drink and then to wait for something
impure but better than St. Sebastian's grace, some
blessedness absolving them of knowledge

and of fear for old Ponce, mad as a hatter in the lists
of dawn, who would lead without followers
if he had to, who made their loyalty a sacred hope.
Against all reason they stared him in the crazed
crossed eyes and said, here is all we have, our youth.
Not quite a fountain, but take it. Take everything.

Mean and Stupid

Ricky Stoppard died
in a slimy, undulant tangle
near the south face of a strip mine
outside Wier, Kansas.
That was where the snakes
caught up to him, praying
too loudly and taking the Lord's name
at the same time.
That was how it was.
All the Baptist farmers
hereabouts will tell you
it was a low-down
two-talking son of a loafing skunk
who died that day (riddance be praised!);
that Ricky stank corn liquor,
cursed life, had once attempted armed robbery
of a charity bazaar in Girard, and that the snakes
were instruments of a judgment
others had been making for a long time before the Almighty
at last threw the machineries of balance
into gear. Rumor
has it, too, that Ricky, when he fell
into the fateful waters of reptilian vengeance,
called out for someone to toss him
a brick; thereby adding stupidity to the list of charges.
I've seen his gravestone and it reads:

RICKY STOPPARD

1953-1985

Mean & Stupid

I'm standing by that stone, and my hat is off
to his silly death
and a life of miserable small crimes
poorly made. I pray I may be spared
the pain and heat of Ricky's soul
that sighed like a rotten wagon wheel
and broke. And I pray for that
soul, the Old Nick of it somehow
near to me as love
or yearning
or any lost equation none of us will ever finally
get. I can hear the night freight
mourning through Riverton
as farmhouse lights die out
below the darker owls circling, flagrantly
disdainful of the Oklahoma line, and Ricky's cruel
headstone comes undone. He's finished now, at least,
and he's all right (being gone). The wind
and blown leaves clatter and agree; at least
he's not all wrong.

Stay with Me

Beautiful arms full with rose starts,
he says a tree
or ship is not a cloudy day.
He says the way wind stains
the brief smiles of doors
is what we get from life
and nothing less or more
should we accept; not even
from strangers, the sometimes holy
and come out of nothing fools.

Who knew he was dying?
We were on the path home
when that bell removed its pearls
and flung them skyward, dozens
of little moons, whole notes, berries
full to sweetness with a song
he sang us from the atmospheres
of Christmas, where all of us are going,
blessed or not,
ready or not, like a grandpa

in a greenhouse humming
and falling into his smile
as we went down the path, away
from the unfractured life; the three
of us filling like glass
with what we were about to know:
this is no dream. Beyond cartwheels
and the slow designs in gray,

every heartbeat is a little morning
with a path and someone,
made almost inarticulate by love,
watching.

The Cry

The moon hangs in alders
by the bridge. Something is crying out
down there in the choked hollow,
down there in the grass. Trapped
or maybe bereft, it trumpets
up the ladders of mist and cold
as if nothing mattered anymore
except voice hefting the exact fullness
of this moment in which something
is terribly wrong.

I'm afraid of you,
whatever you are, and of your grief
or pain sung like a gift
no one will take.
Once, I think I will come down to you
through scotch broom and heaps of leaves
and put my fingers softly
to your throat and stroke you and feel
the dense shiver of language
leaving you, seeking my nameless body
somewhere outside of what we are
in daylight or in summer.
But it's autumn now and I don't want to die
or hear you, dying fascination. I don't
want the frayed rim of your call
ringing back out of my hands
and scuffling shoes. Yet you cannot
be still and the long word rasps
again onto the air.

An owl calls a few times: testing
testing. I turn toward home,
nudging aside pity, guilt, and echoes
of the suffering every creature knows.
Nothing changes what I cannot do.
This is how broken things
pile up inside of me and I keep walking,
calling out, "I love you. Come to me
because I cannot come to you."

The Lover Rejects Himself

On a calm night when terror has left
just about everyone peacefully exhausted,
the thought of an old love touches me
with hands of moonlit snow.
Such pleasure
in the recollection of her clarity of movement!
and of the wet sweetness
now utterly removed from my tongue
and fingers so that I wake from memory
as if a magical grove of orange trees
had grown up in the snow beside me
and disappeared so quickly I say whose
life is this? Is this my sculpted-of-air-and-silver-
indefinite-weight-of-shame? Well, I turn away then,
refusing to breathe
until my fair companion is restored.
See what trouble an old love brings?
See how this moon and snow light may be
the underbelly of death's whiteness,
really?

Brownie Hawkeye

In the last columns of sunlight
holding up the roof
we stood proudly with the fish
so my mother could snap us
and give the attic shoebox this
dusky square-framed happy pittance
of 1955. You can just see
a piece of lake
reflected in my father's casting reel
attached to the pole he holds aloft
like Poseidon lifting his trident
to the powers and bounties of the sea,
that they are his.
And my father's face says

                    on this
tremendous day we struck forth
over dark uncertainties
in an all but rotten boat
and reached down
and brought from the deep a glimmering
alien life
and have returned in the fullness
of our proven skill to this
green eternal shore.

                  It is a shore
gray-yellow now
as I sit gazing, unable
in the vaguely silvered light to tell
if I look back at myself,

at my father beaming there,
or at the fish swinging dead
and beautiful between us.

OK Memory, Let's See What You Can Do on Veteran's Day

Long ago, I was in the Navy, far from home;
a friend and I met a pair of cheerful girls

on the cobbled square in Delft, that ancient
blue-painted porcelain town criss-crossed by canals.

No English on the one side and no Dutch on the other,
it was movie stuff: from a French-windowed public

house wild with girls and sailors to a dance hall
with its slow revolving chandelier of kisses

to a final foggy sweet amazing walk through medieval
streets to where we kissed them once again and gave our word

to find them four days hence upon that very spot
where they rose into the bright bus, assisted by our eyes.

But then some kind of crisis, somewhere, and the ship
pulled out, blankly ignorant of love, and we never even

got to wave or say so long. I can see us now, my friend
and I: flightdeck parade, standing side by stoney side

as the ship steamed down the River Lek and out
into the North Sea. All those years, in my mind,

they've come, two lovely laughing women, and waited
and wondered and gone on into their lives as we did

into ours. And now I think of Maryanne Schraeder
in her forties, still blond, her only son a player

in one of those new wave bands whose music curdles
cream, her husband staying late and later at his work

of repossessing money in the town. And sometimes
Saturday nights she has a few and switches off the lights

and stands in the bluish dark of Europe, looking out
at nothing, and there I am, leaning against a lamppost

in my bulging, splitting, faded dress blues, trying
to light a cigarette. Although I don't smoke them,

the scene's integrity demands I light up and on the third
attempt I get my singed thumbs right and manage it

and tip my whitehat off into a puddle trying to nod,
"Hey Baby, remember me?" And just then she does.

Window

I look out and think of the Brethren
of the Common Life, the love that single gestures must
have shown them as they beat against
the hard peculiarities of Groote's devotions,
and my mind passes over into Deventer,
its moat and ancient spires taking the sunlight
in which Frederick of Heilo and the good
a'Kempis stroll together in their penguinesque cloaks.
                                                             Right here
the Devotio Moderna lights up its collective earnestness
as though five hundred years were glass blown out a window,
pages torn from books.
                          Again Thomas bows
before the sanctity of drovers and shepherds and smiths:
"If you cannot sing like the nightingale
and lark, then sing like the frogs and crows, which sing each
as God intended," he says
in my room here
                              on the budding and breezy plains
where I read *The Imitation of Christ* on my day off, a little
Franz Liszt for background, the active dark
of the pianist's left hand waking a scent of lemons in a Delft bowl
in some everyday life that is not mine.
                                    In fact, after ages
of loving the wrong books, reading women whose syntax was ill-will
itself, whose eyes, when they turned from the fire, were the shapes of fire,
even if I happened to be praying for that, I long for the lemony
precision it is supposed we finally come to.
                                       But it is a long way
to the passions of the good brown scholars, pondering a beast

hemmed in by angels and the extravagance of flesh.

                                     Through my window
I can see blue suggestions of the shriven life
farther from me than a cardinal can fly,

                           farther than the reach
of what we say is honesty or neighborly good hope
or some benison the redbud sprays up to the sweet air
on its knees
dreaming of Liszt, bursting with George Sand.

Bird Love

My wife is on the floor in front
          of the TV set
exercising, her long gorgeous legs

scissoring the grateful air. It is like
          butterflies
filling the room each time her body

unfolds. From the quince outside a cardinal
          looks on, piping time,
utterly in love. And why not love

such plumage as the skin can be? On a morning
          such as this,
after a long night of rain and lightning,

what is more beautiful than a bird
          or a naked woman
bathing in newborn air and in whatever

music she can find? And this love
          the bird in me says
is the exact unsentimental recitation of the breath

and we can't help it. I know. I look at her
          now, foolishly, from my perch
and I can't help singing, simply
          (lift flex kick flex) singing
and I don't care what I sing.

Exclusivity

Orchestral September. The prime
insect quadrillion finish one movement
and crash into the next, mad
with the sexual sweetness of what they are saying.
High in darkened pin oaks
or along the dipping stems of shrubberies
they pipe an ecstasy even the moon could hear
if moon would listen once; if once
she weren't so much the queen
of purest darkness out beyond where sound can go.
So what; the moon has no crickets,
no katydids. So
the moon just watches ripples
of music rising off the lips of the atmosphere,
vaguely stroking her
gravitational tether until, saddened, she seems to burn
a little brighter. Which is what September means
to the insects. I remember
touching you, rubbing
you slowly with this brightness,
the brightness of time. You sang,
I remember, just as the night, because it is the moon's friend,
wished you to, just as the moon does
sing; though we can't hear her.
We can only feel.

Acknowledgements

SOME OF THE POEMS HERE COLLECTED
ORIGINALLY APPEARED IN PERIODICALS
AS FOLLOWS:

∞∞∞

American Literary Review, "Denial," "Lines from a Heaven Imagined by Peaches"; *Carolina Quarterly*, "Ships"; *College English*, "The Abomination of Fallen Things"; *Denver Quarterly*, "Metamorphosis"; *Gettysburg Review*, "The Pipes of Oblivion," "The Contemporary Theorist Alone In His Chair By The Sea," "Window"; *Green Mountain Review*, "Brownie Hawkeye"; *Hubbub*, "The Cry"; *Left Bank*, "The News"; *Local Earth*, "The Ecstasy of Ceasing to Know"; *Midwest Quarterly*, "Mean and Stupid"; *Mississippi Mud*, "The Werewolf at Dawn, The Female Moon Having Left Him"; *Mississippi Review*, "The Blue Flight Back/Adam's Song," "Exclusivity," "Streets," The Record Player"; *North American Review*, "You Sailed Away, Oh Yes You Did"; *North Dakota Quarterly*, "Kipling Visits Portland and the West"; *Northwest Review*, "The God in Central Park," "Night Flight Letter From Weldon Kees," "From the Lover of Violets," "The Christian Science Minotaur," "Blade," "For The Fisherman," "With The Distance," "At Friday Harbor Near Christmas"; *Poetry Northwest*, "Alienation," "Blessing's Precision," "Talk With the Moon," "Bird Love," "The Lover Rejects Himself"; *Portland Review*, "The Ride"; *Willow Springs*, "Out of the Body," "Everyday Dramatics; An Historical Tale," "The Bride of Long Division," "Everything."

"Mean and Stupid" appeared in *A New Geography of Poets*, ed. Edward Field (U. Arkansas Press, Fayetteville), 1992.
"Exclusivity" appeared in *Deep Down Things: Poets of the Inland Northwest*, ed. by McFarland and Schneider (Washington State U. Press, Pullman), 1990.
"The Cry" appeared in *Crossing The River: Poets of the Western United States*, ed. Ray Gonzales (Permanent Press, Sag Harbor, NY), 1987.

ADDITIONALLY:

∞∞∞

"Talk With The Moon" was awarded the Helen Bullis Prize by *Poetry Northwest* in 1991.
"The Cry" was awarded the Vi Gale Award by *Hubbub* in 1988.
"The Bride of Long Division" was awarded the Vachel Lindsay Poetry Prize by *Willow Springs* in 1992.

∞∞∞

The author wishes to extend special thanks to Lex Runciman, Nance Van Winckel, Fred Pfeil, Albert Goldbarth, David Luckert, and Henry Carlile for their generous and intelligent advice concerning this book, and other matters as well.

∞∞∞∞∞

Christopher Howell is author of six collections of poems, most recently Memory and Heaven, and has received grant awards from the National Endowment, the Oregon Arts Commission, and the Massachusetts Council for the Arts. His poems have been widely anthologized and have appeared in many journals, including Hudson Review, The Iowa Review, Poetry Northwest, and The Gettysburg Review. He is principal literary editor for Lynx House Press and coordinator/editor for the Bluestem Award Competition.

EWU
P·R·E·S·S

EASTERN WASHINGTON UNIVERSITY PRESS
SHOWALTER HALL, MS-133
526 5TH STREET, CHENEY WA, 99004-2431

Author photo by Nicole DeVito
Cover design by John Smith
Book layout by Terry Bain